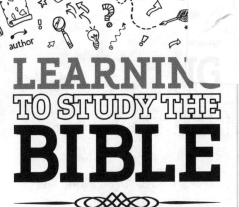

LEARNING TO STUDY THE BIBLE

M000030901

L. J. Zimmerman . . . . .Editor
Theresa Kuhr. . . . . .Production Editor
Arvis Guilbault . . . . Designer

ADMINISTRATIVE TEAM

Rev. Brian K. Milford . . . . President and Publisher
Marjorie M. Pon . . Associate Publisher and Editor of
Church School Publications (CSP)
Mary M. Mitchell. . . . . Design Manager
Brittany Sky . . . Senior Editor, Children's Resources

Written by: L. J. Zimmerman
Cover Design: Kellie Green; **Art:** Shutterstock®

LEARNING TO STUDY THE BIBLE: STUDENT JOURNAL. An official resource for The United Methodist Church approved by Discipleship Ministries and published by Abingdon Press, a division of The United Methodist Publishing House, 2222 Rosa L. Parks Blvd., PO Box 280988, Nashville, TN 37228-0988. Price: $6.99. Copyright © 2018 Abingdon Press. All rights reserved. Printed in the United States of America.

18 19 20 21 22 23 24 25 26 27—10 9 8 7 6 5 4 3 2 1
ISBN: 9781501856273
PACP10526751-01

Who Wrote the Bible?

Well, that's an interesting question.

Let's start with the basics. **The Bible isn't just one book.** It's actually a collection of books—like a library. Sixty-six books, to be exact.

Does that mean there were sixty-six authors of the Bible? Not exactly.

Some books are collections of stories that used to be passed down orally. Before they were written down, people told the stories around fires, at meals, and before bed. The stories were well-known, and everyone told them in a slightly different way. It would be nearly impossible to identify the true "author" of these stories. Instead, we call the person who wrote all the stories down the "editor."

Another thing that makes it hard to tell exactly how many people wrote the Bible is pseudonyms. Pseudonyms are false names. People might use the name of a more famous person to give their writing an extra boost in popularity. One example is in the Book of Ecclesiastes. The author claims to be a king of Israel, implying King Solomon, who was known for his wisdom. But evidence suggests that the book was probably written hundreds of years after King Solomon lived.

Pseudonyms weren't always meant to deceive people. Sometimes a prophet would gather followers. They learned from the prophet and began to think and speak like the prophet. After the prophet's death, his followers might continue writing under his name. This wasn't considered lying. They were simply carrying on the prophet's "train of thought." Parts of the Book of Isaiah are thought to be written by one of Isaiah's followers, years after Isaiah first preached.

As you can tell, there's not a lot we can say for sure about the people who wrote the Bible. All we can do is make our best guess. But there are some things we CAN say with certainty. The people who wrote the Bible had powerful encounters with God. Their lives were changed by their faith, and they wanted to pass their faith on to future generations. That's you!

geography

archaeology

context

language

genre

author

Behind the Texts

Here are some text conversations recovered from a random individual's phone. What can you tell me about this person, just based on their text conversations?

Dinner's ready.

Mom, I'm just upstairs.

You didn't answer when I called.

Oops, my bad. Had my headphones in. What's for dinner?

Mac and cheese. You better come quick or your sister will eat it all.

She's only two.

She's hungry.

K, I'm coming.

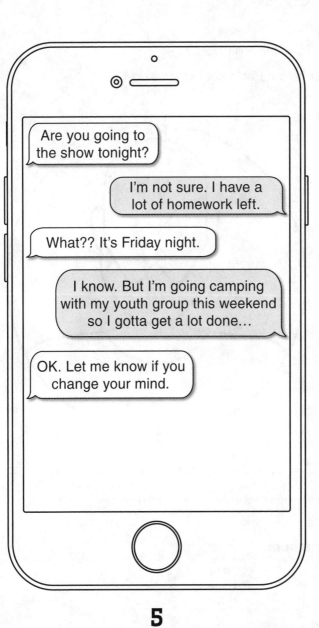

Are you going to the show tonight?

I'm not sure. I have a lot of homework left.

What?? It's Friday night.

I know. But I'm going camping with my youth group this weekend so I gotta get a lot done…

OK. Let me know if you change your mind.

geography

archaeology

context

language

genre

author

Bible Person Profile

Find out more about Paul by checking out these Scriptures:

- Acts 7:54—8:3
- Acts 9:1-20
- 2 Corinthians 11:22-27

Now, fill out Paul's social media profile:

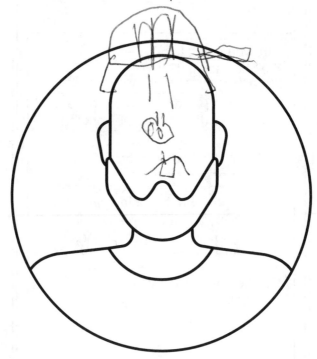

Name:

Paul

Hometown:

samaria

Work History:

scavenging a dumpster for priceless stuff

Hobbies:

Likes:

Dislikes:

geography

archaeology

context

language

genre

author

Journal

Does learning about the people who wrote the Bible change how you see the Scriptures? Why or why not?

author

language

genre

context

archaeology

geography

What Is the Bible, Anyway?

What kind of book is the Bible? Or, more accurately, what kinds of *books* are in the Bible? (Remember when we talked about how the Bible is really a collection of 66 books?!) What section of a bookstore or a library do you think you would find each book of the Bible in, if they were separated?

These questions are all about **genre**, or the category a piece of writing belongs to. The books of the Bible come from many different genres—poetry, narrative, history, personal letters, and more. We can tell a book's genre by reading it carefully and looking for clues. Just like today we know a story that starts out "Once upon a time ..." is a fairy tale, in biblical times,

author

language

genre

context

archaeology

geography

10

authors had their own ways of signaling what genre they were using.

Why does it matter what genre a book is? Well, knowing the genre of a book can completely change our interpretation of it. For example, if we thought a fairy tale was a news report, we might become frightened and end up building ogre-defense systems in our homes, missing the point of the story. Or, if we thought a list of telephone numbers was a secret code, we might spend hours trying to figure it out! Genre is important because it tells you how to understand and respond to a piece of writing.

geography

archaeology

context

language

genre

author

Category Clues

Discovering the genre of a text is a bit like being a detective—it's all about clues. Let's make a list of clues to identify different genres, or categories of writing.

List all the ways you can tell if something is:

a poem

a letter

a sermon

a fiction story

a play

a non-fiction story

a parody

geography

archaeology

context

language

genre

author

Translating Genre

Did you know that the original Hebrew text of the Old Testament didn't have vowels, capitalization, punctuation, verse numbers, or formatting? Check it out:

שמע ישראל יהוה אלהינו יהוה אחד ואהבת את
יהוה אלהיך בכל לבבר ובכל נפשך ובכל מאדך והיו
הדברים האלה אשר אנכי מצוך היום על לבבך ושננתם
לבניך ודברת בב בשבתך בביתך ובלכתך בדרך
ובשכבך ובקומך וקשרתם לאות על ידך והיו לטטפת
בין עיניך וכתבתם על מזזות ביתך ובשעריך
והיה אם שמע תשמעו אל מצותי אשר אנכי
מצוה אתכם היום לאהבה את יהוה אלהיכם ולעבדו
בכל לבבכם ובכל נפשכם ונתתי מטר ארצכם בעתו
יורה ומלקוש ואספת דגנך תירשך ויצהרך ונתתי
עשב בשדך לבהמתך ואכלת ושבעת השמרו לכם
פן יפתה לבבכם וסרתם ועבדתם אלהים אחרים
והשתחויתם להם וחרה אף יהוה בכם ועצר את
השמים ולא יהיה מטר והאדמה לא תתן את יבולה
ואבדתם מהרה מעל הארץ הטבה אשר יהוה נתן לכם
ושמתם את דברי אלה על לבבכם ועל נפשכם וקשרתם
אתם לאות על ידכם והיו לטוטפת בין עיניכם ולמדתם
אתם את בניכם לדבר בם בשבתך בביתך ובלכתך
בדרך ובשכבך ובקומך וכתבתם על מזוזות ביתך
ובשעריך למען ירבו ימיכם וימי בניכם על האדמה
אשר נשבע יהוה לאבתיכם לתת להם כימי השמים
על הארץ

Vowels and paragraph divisions were added to the Hebrew text between the sixth and tenth centuries—hundreds of years after the original texts were written. The chapter and verse numbers we use today were added in the twelfth century. All the rest of the punctuation—indents, question marks, quotation marks, and everything else—is up to modern translators to decide.

These details are important because vocabulary, punctuation, and formatting are major clues to genre. Check out Jonah,

Chapter 2, in two different translations of the Bible—the Common English Bible and the King James Version. What differences do you notice between each version? How did each translator communicate the genre of the passage, as he or she saw it? Which interpretation do you agree with?

Why don't you give it a try yourself? Take the following text from Jonah 1:7b-10. Add your own punctuation, formatting, and verse numbers. Then compare it to what's printed in your Bibles!

THEY CAST LOTS AND THE LOT FELL ON

JONAH SO THEY SAID TO HIM TELL US

SINCE YOU'RE THE CAUSE OF THIS EVIL

HAPPENING TO US WHAT DO YOU DO AND

WHERE ARE YOU FROM WHAT'S YOUR

COUNTRY AND OF WHAT PEOPLE ARE YOU

HE SAID TO THEM I'M A HEBREW I WORSHIP

THE LORD THE GOD OF HEAVEN WHO MADE

THE SEA AND THE DRY LAND THEN THE

MEN WERE TERRIFIED AND SAID TO HIM

WHAT HAVE YOU DONE THE MEN KNEW

THAT JONAH WAS FLEEING FROM THE LORD

BECAUSE HE HAD TOLD THEM

Journal

Figuring out the genre of a part of the Bible is important, but it's often a guessing game. How do you feel about the possibility of mistaking the genre of a book? How important is it for you to know what the original author meant? Do you think the Bible can change genres and meanings over time? Why or why not?

author

language

genre

context

archaeology

geography

Contextualize It

context (noun) \kän-tekst\ | the group of conditions that exist where and when something happens. From the Latin *contextere*, "to weave together."

What's up? What's down? What's going on around you? Are you a fish swimming in a pond? Are you a bird flying in the air? Are you a snail sliding along the ground, oozing a trail of goo? Whatever is happening in your world, whatever circumstances affect your everyday life, that's your "historical context."

In most American cities, our context includes things like

- the fact that you can take a car or bus to school;
- the ability to instantly get in touch with people hundreds of miles away through e-mail and phones;
- the fact that most kids in your community—both boys and girls—learn how to read; and
- the ability to buy fresh fruits and vegetables from the grocery store all year round.

These realities are so common that many people don't realize that they haven't always been true, and still aren't true in every culture. For most people, their context feels like "the way things should be." They don't even realize there's another way of doing things until they meet someone from another culture.

When we read the Bible, we're like time travelers entering another culture. We're reading stories, prophecies, and letters from completely different contexts, passed down to us through hundreds of years. Nobody reading the Bible today remembers what it was like to live in Jerusalem when King David ruled, or in Persia when Esther was queen, or in Nazareth when Jesus was growing up.

So, when we read the Bible today, we have to work extra hard to "contextualize" it. That means we have to put the story back in its own context. First, we learn about the time and place where the story was written, so we can understand what it might have meant at the time. We also put the story in its literary context by reading what comes before and after the story. Then, we can think about what it might mean today, in our own context.

author

Alien Archaeologist

Imagine you're an alien from a distant planet. You've just completed your first successful space travel mission and landed on Earth. You begin exploring and encounter the following objects/items. Write what you think each item might be for. Remember, you know absolutely NOTHING about human culture.

language

genre

context

hair straightener

archaeology

carousel

geography

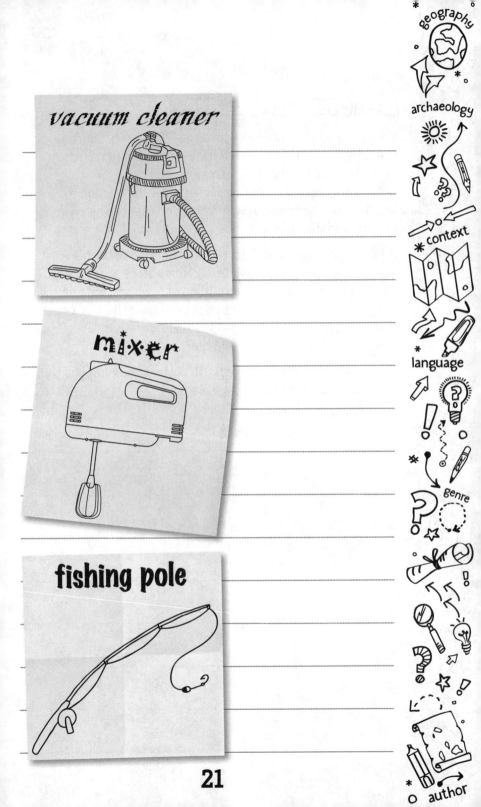

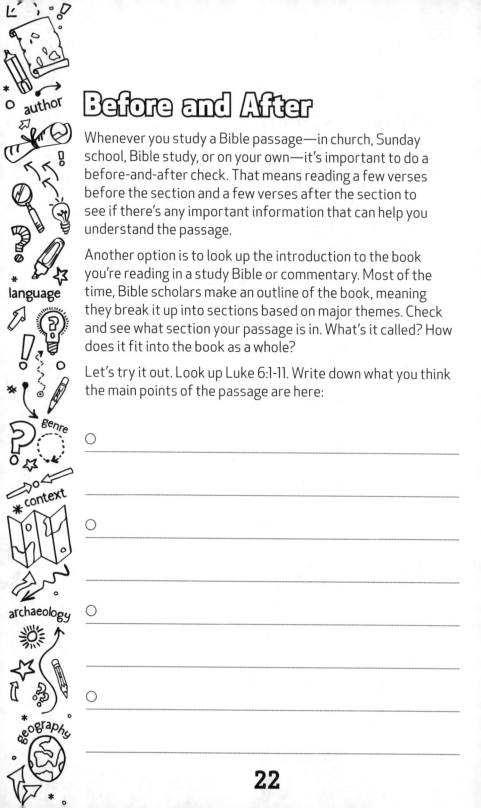

Before and After

Whenever you study a Bible passage—in church, Sunday school, Bible study, or on your own—it's important to do a before-and-after check. That means reading a few verses before the section and a few verses after the section to see if there's any important information that can help you understand the passage.

Another option is to look up the introduction to the book you're reading in a study Bible or commentary. Most of the time, Bible scholars make an outline of the book, meaning they break it up into sections based on major themes. Check and see what section your passage is in. What's it called? How does it fit into the book as a whole?

Let's try it out. Look up Luke 6:1-11. Write down what you think the main points of the passage are here:

○ _____

_____

○ _____

_____

○ _____

_____

○ _____

_____

author

language

genre

context

archaeology

geography

Now do your before-and-after check. What did you find? How do the sections before and after the passage change your interpretation, if at all?

Before

- _____
- _____
- _____
- _____
- _____
- _____

After

- _____
- _____
- _____
- _____
- _____
- _____

geography

archaeology

context

language

genre

author

Journal

Do you think the Bible can still be meaningful to your daily life when you live in such a different historical context? Why or why not?

author

language

genre

context

archaeology

geography

Bible Geography 101

When you hear the word *geography*, what do you think? If you're like most people, you think of maps. But geography is about much more than national borders or navigation.

The geography, or landscape, of your homeland shapes your life in important ways. Your local geography determines the food you eat, the clothes you wear, the type of house you live in, and more.

Now that we live in a globally connected world, we're not completely limited by our geography. We can eat a banana grown in Jamaica, pull on a T-shirt made in Cambodia, and ride in a car made in Japan—all before we arrive at school. Even so, it's likely that if you live on the Maine coast, seafood is a regular part of your diet; and if you live in Alaska, you own a heavy coat; and if you live in Oklahoma, you know where to take shelter during a tornado.

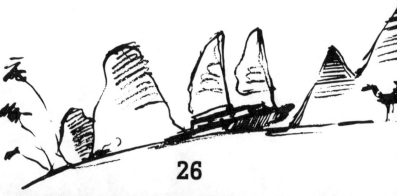

How much our geography affects us differs depending on where we live. But in biblical times, geography played a much bigger role in people's lives. They didn't have cars or planes or telephones. Their lives were determined by their local geography. They ate whatever food they could grow or raise on the land. They wore whatever clothing they could make from local plants or animal skins. They built houses out of bricks made from local mud or stone.

How does biblical geography compare to your local geography? Use the questions on the next page to figure it out!

Your Geo-graph

Okay, so you know that your local geography affects your life. But HOW does your local geography affect your specific life? Answer the questions below to create your very own personalized Geo-graph. Circle all that apply.

I live near:

mountains   rivers
                                      volcanoes
fields   lakes
                                      the jungle
the ocean   forests

The weather where I live is usually:

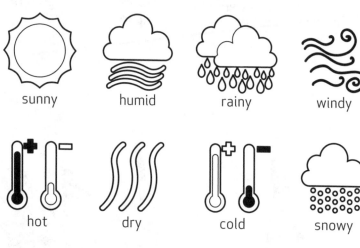

sunny   humid   rainy   windy

hot   dry   cold   snowy

We have to watch out for:

blizzards   hurricanes   landslides

tornadoes   flash floods   volcanic eruptions

A food we're famous for is:

Houses where I live tend to look like this:

Most of my clothes are made out of:

cotton   wool   polyester

linen   leather   some other fabric

Biblical Landscape

Most of the stories in the Bible take place in Israel, a land that was small, but packed with diversity.

The land of ancient Israel contained high mountains (Mount Hermon is 9,000 feet!) as well as the Dead Sea, which is the lowest point on the earth's surface. Parts of Israel were dry and desert-like, and other parts were humid and close to the Mediterranean Sea.

author

language

genre

context

archaeology

geography

Wheat, barley, figs, pistachios, grapes, and olive trees were abundant, which means the Israelites snacked on tasty bread, olive oil, fruit, and nuts.

Sheep and goats were able to survive on the dry, broken terrain, so Israelite clothes were often made from wool or leather.

Journal

Now that you know more about the wilderness the Israelites wandered in, it's time to interpret the story. What does the wilderness symbolize to you? Have you ever been in a spiritual wilderness?

author

language

genre

context

archaeology

geography

Layers and Lenses

There are **layers to interpretation.** There are also lenses. Lenses and layers. Layers and lenses. How do you keep track of all those *L*'s? Here's a breakdown of the lenses and layers of Bible interpretation:

Layers

Between the original author and the modern reader, the Bible passes through many hands. By the time the Bible gets to you, it's already gone through several layers of interpretation, which have influenced the meaning.

1. **The Translators**—The Bible was originally written in Hebrew, Greek, and occasionally other languages. You can read the Bible in English thanks to the work of translators. If you've ever learned a foreign language, you know that translation can be tricky. Words and phrases in one language don't translate neatly into another. Take the English phrase "I ran into him at the store." If you translated that word-by-word into another language, the reader might imagine someone literally sprinting into another person. In order to get the true meaning across, the translator needs to figure out how to convey the idea of coincidentally meeting someone at the store. Translators have to decide the best way to communicate all kinds of words and phrases in another language, and that's interpretation.

2. **The Canonizers**—How did the Bible become the Bible? Why were some stories, letters, and gospels preserved while others faded into obscurity? The answer lies with the canonizers. The canonizers are the people who decided which books were important enough to be in the *canon* or the Christian Bible, and what order they should go in. Most of the canonizers were Christian leaders during the second to fourth centuries.

3. **The Scribes**—Back before the printing press was invented, each copy of the Bible was written by hand by a scribe. Scribes carefully wrote every word exactly as they saw it in their original manuscript. But the scribes were human. Sometimes they made mistakes. Sometimes they intentionally altered the text to make up for what they thought was an error. As archaeologists unearth and historians preserve ancient scrolls, they can compare them to discover the variations.

4. **The Editors**—Many of the books of the Bible draw from different sources. The editors of the Bible took many stories, written and passed down orally, and wove them into one story. Biblical scholars can sometimes tell when an editor has combined two stories, because the writing style changes abruptly.

Lenses

In addition to layers, there are also **lenses of interpretation.** Everybody wears metaphorical glasses when they read. The "lenses" you read through influence how you interpret the story. Your lenses are shaped by life experiences. A [▪] short person will have a different lens reading the story of Zacchaeus than a tall person. Someone with an anxiety disorder will read Jesus' encouragement not to worry differently than others. Everyone has a different set of lenses. That's why everyone reads the Bible a little differently!

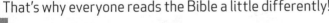

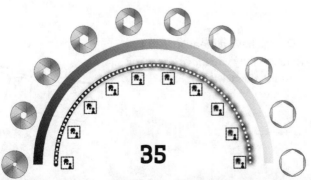

Name Your Lenses

What are you like? How do you see the world? What's your unique perspective? Use the following open-ended questions to begin naming some of your lenses!

Do you speak the same language at home and at school?

Yes

Have you ever felt singled out because of race or ethnicity?

no

Do you feel like there are some activities you should or shouldn't do because of your gender?

no

Are you tall, short, or in-between?

Tall

Do you have a disability that affects how you move, learn, or interact with others?

no

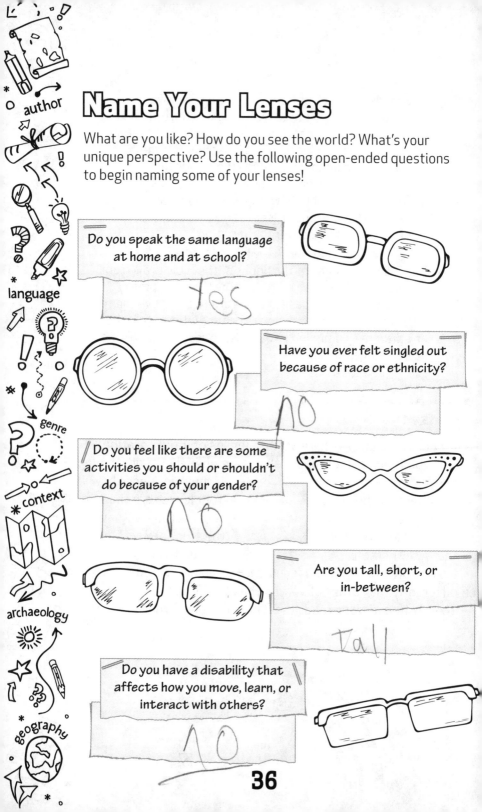

author

language

genre

context

archaeology

geography

Are you an introvert, extrovert, or in-between?

Do you read things from start to finish, or jump around?

Start to finish

Do you feel like you have enough, too much, or too little?

enough

Do you feel like you fit in with your peers?

Yes

Are you the oldest, youngest, middle, or only child?

oldest

How do you want to spend the majority of your time?

Playing video games with friends.

geography

archaeology

context

language

genre

author

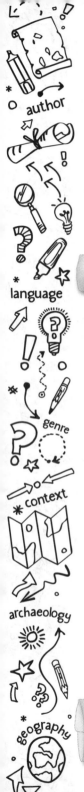

God's Image

Did you know that one of the most debated parts of the Bible is in the very first chapter? Genesis 1 is a poem about Creation. The poet says that God created humanity in "God's own image." For centuries, Jews and Christians have tried to understand what that means. What's your interpretation?

Read Verse 27, and what comes after it, in Genesis 1:27-31.

27God created humanity in God's own image,

in the divine image God created them,

male and female God created them.

28God blessed them and said to them, "Be fertile and multiply; fill the earth and master it. Take charge of the fish of the sea, the birds in the sky, and everything crawling on the ground." 29Then God said, "I now give to you all the plants on the earth that yield seeds and all the trees whose fruit produces its seeds within it. These will be your food. 30To all wildlife, to all the birds in the sky, and to everything crawling on the ground—to everything that breathes—I give all the green grasses for food." And that's what happened. 31God saw everything he had made: it was supremely good. There was evening and there was morning: the sixth day.

Read it from a few different translations so you have a sense of what the original language could have meant. *(The translation printed here is from the Common English Bible.)*

Next, write your initial thoughts about what it means to be made in God's image:

_____

_____

_____

_____

_____

_____

_____

_____

_____

_____

_____

Journal

Now that you've investigated other people's interpretation of the meaning of "God's image," what do YOU think? What does it mean to be created in God's image? How does this passage affect how you see yourself? How you see others?

author

language

genre

context

archaeology

geography

Four Meanings, One Text

How many different ways can you read one passage of the Bible? Well, since the Middle Ages, some Jewish and Christian Bible interpreters have believed there are at least four ways. Their lists didn't match up perfectly, but each tradition listed four unique ways to interpret Scripture. Here's a mash-up of the two lists:

1. The literal, or plain meaning.

Christian interpreters called this the *literal sense*. Rabbis called this the *peshat*, from the Hebrew word for "surface." This way of reading takes the text at face value.

2. The comparative meaning.

The comparative meaning is the meaning passages take on when read in connection with other parts of the Bible. Christian interpreters called this the *allegorical* or *typological sense*. Rabbis called this the *derash*, from the Hebrew

1

2

word for "inquire, seek." This way of reading looks at a passage as a part of the whole Bible, not just by itself.

3. The deeper symbolic meaning.

Christian interpreters called this the *moral sense*, or the "moral of the story." Rabbis called this the *remez*, from the Hebrew word for "hints." This way of reading looks for meaningful symbols and lessons that can be drawn from the passage.

4. The secret, mystical meaning.

Christian interpreters called this the *anagogical sense*. They believed some passages contained hidden prophecies about heaven, hell, and the second coming of Christ. Rabbis called this the *sod*, from the Hebrew word for "secret." They believed this meaning of the text could only be revealed to a reader through divine inspiration.

Interpret a Fairy Tale

Let's try out the first three forms of interpretation with a common story—"Little Red Riding Hood." If it's been a while since you've heard the story, here's a recap:

Little Red Riding Hood is a little girl named after the fancy, red cloak she wears. One day, her mother sends her to visit her granny with a basket of food. Her mother warns her to stay on the path through the forest.

A Big Bad Wolf is also in the forest. He spies Red and follows her for a while. He approaches her and asks her where she's going. Red tells the Wolf she's visiting her granny. The Wolf suggests that she pick some flowers for Granny. While Red is picking flowers, the Wolf goes ahead of her and eats her granny!

The Wolf puts on Granny's clothes and waits for Red to arrive. Red notices immediately how different Granny looks. She comments, "My, what big eyes you have!" The Wolf responds, "The better to see you with, my dear." Red says, "My, what big ears you have!" The Wolf responds, "The better to hear you with, my dear." Red exclaims, "My, what big teeth you have!" The Wolf growls, "The better to eat you with!" then proceeds to eat Red as well. Fortunately, a hunter drops by, cuts open the Big Bad Wolf, and rescues Little Red Riding Hood and her granny.

1. **Literal meaning**—tell the story in your own words to your partner (or whoever is around).

_____

_____

_____

_____

2. **Comparative meaning**—are there any connections between this story and other fairy tales? Do Big Bad Wolves appear in other stories? What about young girls? Grandmothers? Forests? Think of all the connections you can.

_____

_____

_____

_____

3. **Symbolic meaning**—What's the "moral of the story?" What are the symbols in the story? What do they represent?

_____

_____

_____

_____

geography

archaeology

context

language

genre

author

Captain Obvious

When you're interpreting the literal sense of a biblical passage, you can feel like Captain Obvious. You're just saying the same thing in your own words. You're stating the obvious.

That's okay! That's an important part of Bible study. Because the truth is, most of the time the *literal meaning* of the text IS obvious. But sometimes it isn't. It's always good to check for a basic level of understanding by restating the main points of the passage in your own words. If that exercise isn't easy, you may need to do some more research to understand the literal sense of the text.

It's your turn to be Captain Obvious. Check out the story in Genesis 22:1-19. Then answer these basic questions:

1. Who is in the story?

_____

_____

_____

2. Where does the story take place?

_____

_____

_____

3. What are the main points of the plot?

_____

_____

_____

4. How does the story end?

_____

_____

_____

geography

archaeology

context

language

genre

author

Journal

Now that you've explored the first three senses of the story, it's time to explore the "secret sense." What does this story in Genesis 22:1-19 mean to you? What is God saying to you through this story? What special meaning does it hold for you?

author

language

genre

context

archaeology

geography

Divine Reading

Over the past few weeks, you've learned a ton about how the Bible was created. You've explored who wrote it, what kinds of writings are in it, when and where it was created, and why all of that matters. You've learned about layers and lenses of interpretation, and four senses of Scripture. Your Bible knowledge is expanding rapidly!

Now it's time to shift the focus. Let's talk about YOU. Yes, you. The Bible isn't just about the people who created it. If it were, why would we still be reading it after all these years? The Bible is also about you. It's your sacred story, and it's your life that is affected by how you relate to the Bible.

When you pick up the Bible, you're not just reading about your spiritual ancestors' encounters with God. You're also opening yourself to having your own encounter with God. The Holy Spirit speaks to us in many ways, and one of those ways is through the words of the Bible.

Today we're going to investigate where you are in the biblical story. What is God saying to YOU through the Bible? How can YOU get closer to Christ through reading Scripture?

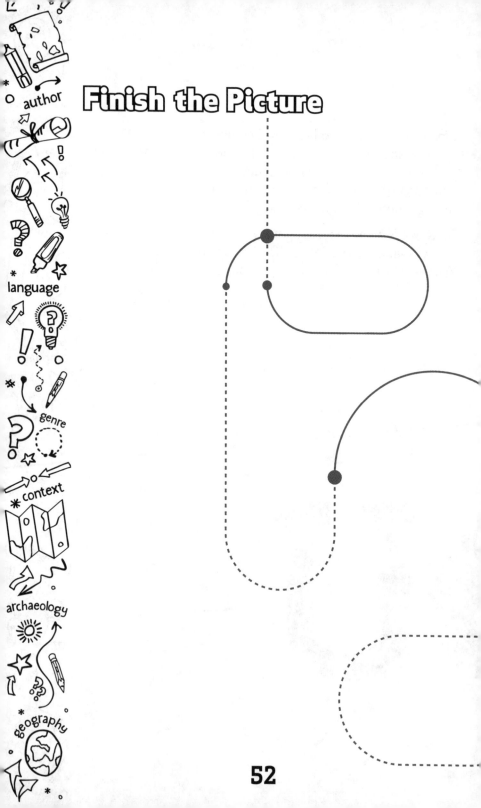

Finish the Picture

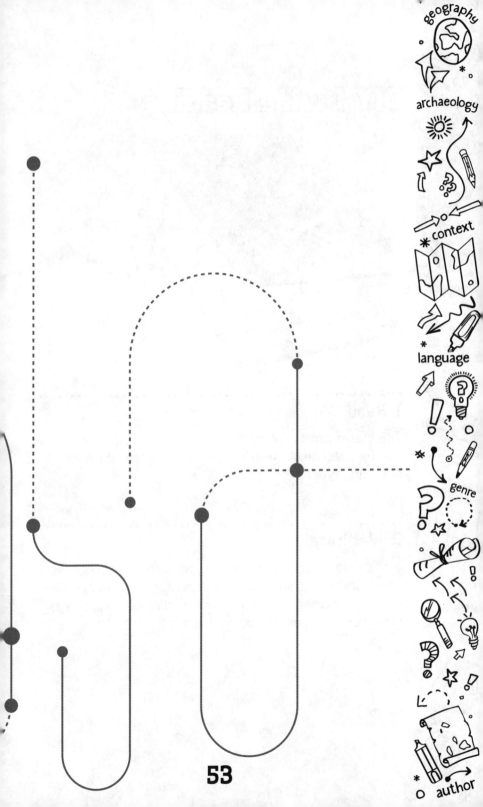

DIY Divine Reading

1. Read

This step is pretty straightforward. Read the passage carefully. Notice any words or phrases that "shimmer" or stick out in your mind.

2. Meditate

In this step, let your brain get creative with the passage. As you or someone else reads the passage again, draw or paint whatever images come to you, rewrite a verse, or doodle as you go over the passage in your mind.

3. Pray

In this step, talk to God as you read the passage. You can read the passage as though you're praying it, or you can talk to God about what the passage means to you today. You can simply ask, "God, what are you saying to me through this passage today?"

4. Contemplate

In this step, listen for God's response to your prayer and meditation. As someone reads the passage a final time, quiet your mind and be open to any response you sense. You might want to have something to keep your hands busy while you contemplate, like meditation beads.

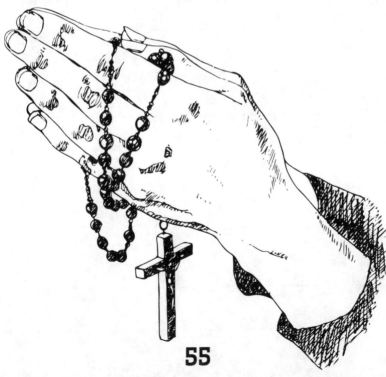

Journal

What did you hear from God as you practiced divine reading today? How will you respond to what you heard?

author

language

genre

context

archaeology

geography

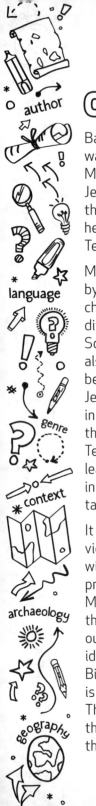

Canon Connections

Back in the days of the early church, being called a "Marcionite" was a big insult. Marcionites followed a guy named Marcion, who argued that the teachings of Jesus were completely incompatible with the God of the Old Testament. Thus, he believed that the God of the Old Testament could not be Jesus' father.

Marcion's teachings were rejected by the early church. Even though church leaders recognized some differences between the Hebrew Scriptures and the Gospels, they also saw deep connections. They believed that the teachings of Jesus built upon the teachings in the Hebrew Scriptures. Rather than throwing out the Old Testament, early church leaders reinterpreted it in light of what Jesus taught.

It can be tempting to view the Bible as one epic story, with a plot that perfectly progresses with each book. Marcion thought that's what the Bible should be, so he threw out the parts that didn't match his idea of the biblical story. But the Bible isn't one big story. The Bible is more like one big conversation. There are diverse perspectives, and they don't always easily fit together. But the many voices of the Bible help us understand the many angles of truth.

The parts of the Bible that don't seem to fit are often just another way of looking at the same truth. For many Jews, it didn't seem possible to say that a person was God, or even the Son of God. That concept just didn't fit into their understanding of God. But Christians said that it was possible. They reinterpreted the Hebrew Scriptures in light of Jesus and found new meanings.

Today, Christians read the New Testament alongside the Old Testament all the time. Some churches follow a schedule of Scripture readings for worship each Sunday. That schedule is called a **lectionary**. The lectionary always has readings from the Old and New Testaments, because Christians believe the Old and New Testaments talk to each other. Scripture is a conversation, and each Sunday we get to explore different parts of that conversation through the lectionary.

geography

archaeology

context

language

genre

author

Musical Conversations

Inter-textual conversations don't just happen in the Bible. They happen all the time in popular music. Sometimes, musicians use tunes or lyrical phrases from songs that came before them to create new songs. This is called *sampling*. Other times, musicians combine two songs into one new song. This is called a *mash-up*. In a mash-up, two songs that were unrelated before have a "conversation" and take on new meaning.

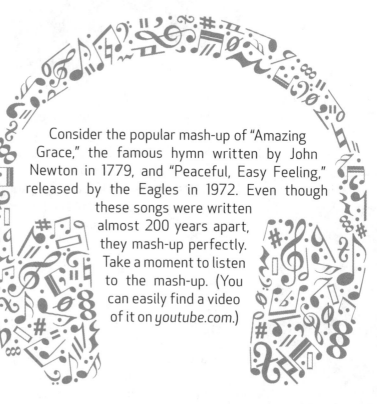

Consider the popular mash-up of "Amazing Grace," the famous hymn written by John Newton in 1779, and "Peaceful, Easy Feeling," released by the Eagles in 1972. Even though these songs were written almost 200 years apart, they mash-up perfectly. Take a moment to listen to the mash-up. (You can easily find a video of it on *youtube.com*.)

"Peaceful, Easy Feeling" is about romantic love, but when it's mashed up with "Amazing Grace," it becomes a beautiful reflection on God's love. The mash-up reminds Christians that even though romantic love is important, the love of God is the "solid ground" that we stand on.

Can you think of other songs that use tunes or words from another song? Can you think of other examples of mash-ups of two or more songs? What two songs do you think would make a good mash-up? Why?

_____

_____

_____

_____

_____

_____

_____

Conversations are happening all around you—even in your headphones! Listen for more musical conversations as you enjoy your favorite tunes this week.

The LORD Is My Shepherd

Psalm 23 is what you might call a classic. Chances are, you've heard it before. You may even have memorized it when you were younger. Take a moment to refresh your memory:

> ¹*The LORD is my shepherd.*
>   *I lack nothing.*
> ²*He lets me rest in grassy meadows;*
>   *he leads me to restful waters;*
>   ³*he keeps me alive.*
> *He guides me in proper paths*
>   *for the sake of his good name.*
>
> ⁴*Even when I walk through the darkest valley,*
>   *I fear no danger because you are with me.*
> *Your rod and your staff—*
>   *they protect me.*
>
> ⁵*You set a table for me*
>   *right in front of my enemies.*
> *You bathe my head in oil;*
>   *my cup is so full it spills over!*
> ⁶*Yes, goodness and faithful love*
>   *will pursue me all the days of my life,*
>   *and I will live in the LORD's house*
>   *as long as I live.*

Did you know that one of the prophets sampled from Psalm 23? Ezekiel 34:1-16 uses this image of God as Israel's shepherd to speak out against unjust leaders. Check out verses 11-16.

> [11]*The Lᴏʀᴅ God proclaims: I myself will search for my flock and seek them out.* [12]*As a shepherd seeks out the flock when some in the flock have been scattered, so will I seek out my flock. I will rescue them from all the places where they were scattered during the time of clouds and thick darkness.* [13]*I will gather and lead them out from the countries and peoples, and I will bring them to their own fertile land. I will feed them on Israel's highlands, along the riverbeds, and in all the inhabited places.* [14]*I will feed them in good pasture, and their sheepfold will be there, on Israel's lofty highlands. On Israel's highlands, they will lie down in a secure fold and feed on green pastures.* [15]*I myself will feed my flock and make them lie down. This is what the Lᴏʀᴅ God says.* [16]*I will seek out the lost, bring back the strays, bind up the wounded, and strengthen the weak. But the fat and the strong I will destroy, because I will tend my sheep with justice.*

What connections do you see between Ezekiel 34:11-16 and Psalm 23? What do those connections teach you about God?

_____

_____

_____

_____

geography
archaeology
context
language
genre
author

Journal

Does thinking of the Bible as a conversation rather than a story change how you interact with it? Do you see yourself as a part of the biblical conversation? Why or why not?

_____

_____

_____

_____

_____

_____

_____

_____

_____

_____

_____

author

language

genre

context

archaeology

geography